SOUND

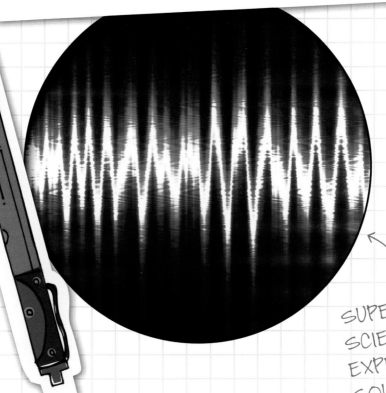

by Christine Taylor-Butler

CHERRY LAKE PUBLISHING • ANN ARBOR, MICHIGAN

A NOTE TO PARENTS AND TEACHERS: Please review the instructions for these experiments before your children do them. Be sure to help them with any experiments you do not think they can safely conduct on their own.

A NOTE TO KIDS: Be sure to ask an adult for help with these experiments when you need it. Always put your safety first!

Published in the United States of America by
Cherry Lake Publishing
Ann Arbor, Michigan
www.cherrylakepublishing.com

Content Editor: Robert Wolffe, EdD,
Professor of Teacher Education,
Bradley University, Peoria, Illinois

Book design and illustration: The Design Lab

Photo Credits: Cover and page 1, ©Argus456/Dreamstime.com;
page 7, ©Joseph, used under license from Shutterstock, Inc.; page 8,
©iStockphoto.com/EricHood; page 12, ©sonya etchison, used under
license from Shutterstock, Inc.; page 16, ©MANDY GODBEHEAR, used
under license from Shutterstock, Inc.; page 20, ©iStockphoto.com/
bdphotos; page 24, ©Rasento/Dreamstime.com

Library of Congress Cataloging-in-Publication Data
Taylor-Butler, Christine.
  Super cool science experiments: Sound / by Christine Taylor-Butler.
      p. cm.—(Science explorer)
  Includes bibliographical references and index.
  ISBN-13: 978-1-60279-532-7   ISBN-10: 1-60279-532-0 (lib. bdg.)
  ISBN-13: 978-1-60279-611-9   ISBN-10: 1-60279-611-4 (pbk.)
  1. Sound—Experiments—Juvenile literature. I. Title. II. Title: Sound.
III. Series.
  QC225.5.T39 2010
  534.078—dc22   2009006010

Cherry Lake Publishing would like to acknowledge the work
of The Partnership for 21st Century Skills. Please visit
www.21stcenturyskills.org for more information.

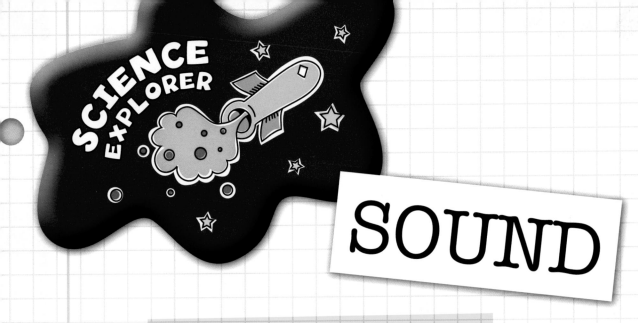

SOUND

TABLE OF CONTENTS

Listen Up!

Beep! There goes your alarm. It's time to get ready for school. Chirp, Chirp, Chirp! Birds are singing outside your window. Ding! Your father is making oatmeal in the microwave for breakfast. These are just a few of the sounds you might hear before you've even gotten out of bed. You'll hear many more sounds throughout your day. Sounds are everywhere.

Have you ever wondered how you are able to hear something? Or how sounds are made in the first place? If so, you have the curiosity of a scientist. Want to learn more about sound? You can do experiments with things you already have at home. In this book, we'll learn how scientists think. We'll do that by experimenting with sound. We'll see just how much fun it is to design our own experiments and learn new things about sound!

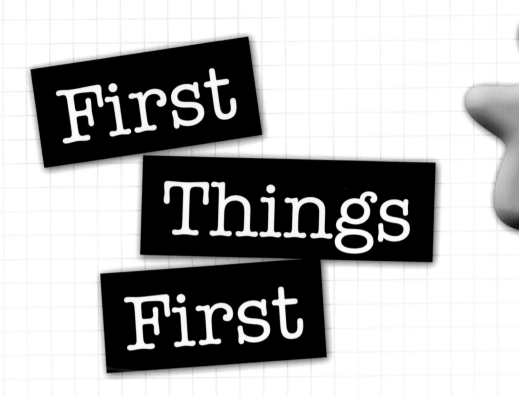

First Things First

Scientists learn by studying something very carefully. For example, scientists who study sound measure how far sounds travel. They learn how sounds change in the environment. They notice which sounds humans can hear and which ones they cannot. They do experiments to test how sound can be used in daily life.

Good scientists take notes on everything they discover. They write down their observations. Sometimes those observations lead scientists to ask new questions. With new questions in mind, they design experiments to find the answers.

When scientists design experiments, they must think very clearly. The way they think about problems is often called the scientific method. What is the scientific method? It's a step-by-step way of

finding answers
to specific questions.
The steps don't always follow
the same pattern. Sometimes
scientists change their minds. The process
Scientific often works something like this:
method

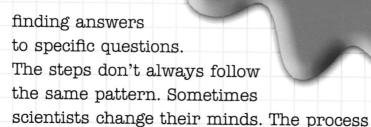

- **Step One:** A scientist gathers the facts and makes observations about one particular thing.
- **Step Two:** The scientist comes up with a question that is not answered by all the observations and facts.
- **Step Three:** The scientist creates a hypothesis. This is a statement of what the scientist thinks is probably the answer to the question.
- **Step Four:** The scientist tests the hypothesis. He or she designs an experiment to see whether the hypothesis is correct. The scientist does the experiment and writes down what happens.
- **Step Five:** The scientist draws a conclusion based on how the experiment turned out. The conclusion might be that the hypothesis is correct. Sometimes, though, the hypothesis is not correct. In that case, the scientist might develop a new hypothesis and another experiment.

In the following experiments, we'll see the scientific method in action. We'll gather some facts and observations about sound. And for each experiment, we'll develop a question and a hypothesis. Next, we'll do an actual experiment to see if our hypothesis is correct. By the end of the experiment, we should know something new about sound. Scientists, are you ready? Then let's get started!

Listen up! Let's learn about sound.

Experiment #1
The Drum in Your Ear

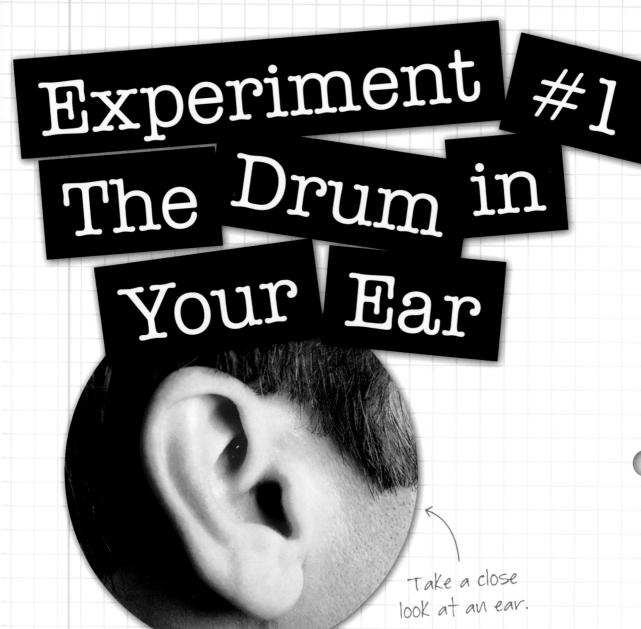

Take a close look at an ear.

First, let's gather some observations. What do you already know about sound? You know that sounds are all around us. Some sounds are very soft. They can be difficult to hear. Other sounds are loud enough to hurt your ears. Have you ever been in a car with loud music playing? Some car stereos can produce sounds that are loud enough to rattle the car's windows—or even your body. Have you ever placed your hand against a stereo speaker? The speaker vibrates when the bass is turned up.

These observations lead us to a question. Does sound contain an invisible source of energy? Could this energy produce some type of change in an object? Could it cause something to move? Come up with a hypothesis about how sound can act on an object. Here is one possibility: **Sound can be used to make something move.** Now you can set up an experiment to test the hypothesis.

Here's what you'll need:

- A roll of clear plastic food wrap
- An empty bowl
- 2 large rubber bands
- A roll of tape
- ¼ teaspoon of rice
- A metal cookie sheet
- A wooden spoon
- A whistle

These materials should be easy to find

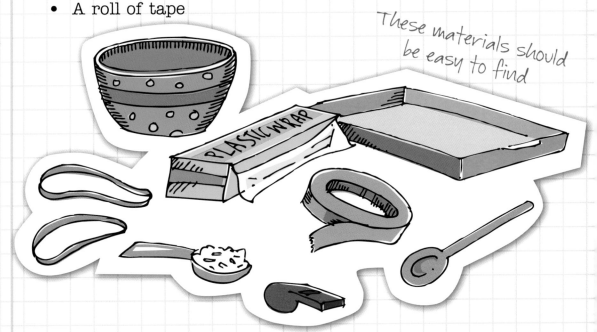

Instructions:

1. Stretch the plastic wrap over the top of your bowl. Use the rubber bands to hold the wrap tight against the bowl. If the rubber bands are not large enough to stretch across the rim of the bowl, you can use tape.

What do you think will happen to the rice?

2. Sprinkle the rice on top of the wrap.
3. Clap your hands above the bowl. Your hands should be close to the bowl, but not touching it. What happens to the rice?
4. Hold the cookie sheet 1 inch (2.5 centimeters) above the bowl. Bang the cookie sheet with the wooden spoon. What do you observe?
5. Try blowing the whistle near the plastic wrap. What do you observe this time?
6. Stand with your face 2 inches (5.1 cm) above the bowl. Shout as loud as you can. What happens to the rice?

Conclusion:

What happened to the rice when you made different sounds? Did it move about? The sounds you made sent vibrations through the air. These vibrations are sound waves. The sound waves caused the plastic wrap to vibrate. The vibrating plastic made the rice jump. Does this help explain why the rice moved when you made different noises? What conclusion can you make from your experiment? Did you prove your hypothesis?

Your ear contains a thin layer of skin called an eardrum. The eardrum vibrates when it is exposed to sound. Tiny hairs behind the eardrum convert these sound vibrations into electrical impulses that your brain can understand. Noises that are too loud can damage hair cells or your hearing nerve. Scientists think that the force of vibrations from a very loud sound can damage your hearing. So never expose your ears to loud sounds for more than a few seconds, if at all. You could permanently damage the sensitive structures in your ears and lose your hearing.

Experiment #2 Make Waves!

Do you need to be this close to hear someone speak?

In Experiment #1, we learned that sound causes vibrations. These vibrations contain enough energy to make small objects move. But how does sound travel through the air? Think in terms of direction. Does sound travel in a straight line? In all directions? Think about talking with a friend. Can you only hear your friend if she is talking directly in your ear? Are you able to hear her even if she is behind you, in front of you, or to your side at different angles? Come up with a hypothesis. Here is one option: **Sound travels in a straight line.**

Here's what you'll need:
- A cake pan or pie pan
- Water
- A dropper

You probably have all of these things in your kitchen.

Instructions:
1. Fill the pan halfway with water.
2. Fill the dropper with water.
3. Hold the dropper 3 inches (7.6 cm) above the pan.

4. Squeeze the bulb of the dropper to release a drop of water into the center of the pan. What happens?
5. Wait for the water in the pan to settle. Then release another drop. Again, observe what happens.

Squeeze just hard enough to release one drop of water.

Conclusion:
The pan of water represents air. The drop hitting the water represents the source of a sound. The ripples represent sound waves. In which direction do the waves travel? Do they seem to be spreading in all directions? Was your hypothesis correct? Don't be discouraged if your hypothesis is wrong. Exciting discoveries often come from unexpected results!

Vibrations push against the water molecules to make a wave that moves away from an object in all directions. Sound works in a similar way. That is why you can hear a person speak, even if he is facing away from you. The air is also made up of tiny molecules. A sound vibration pushes against the molecules. These molecules bump into other molecules, which bump into more molecules. This forms a wave. As the molecules hit one another, they lose energy. That is why a noise sounds louder if you are standing close to the source and softer if you are standing far away. Although water was used here to demonstrate how sound waves travel, there are actually important differences between the behavior of sound and water waves.

In 1886, a German scientist discovered a way to send and receive sound waves through a radio transmitter. Heinrich Hertz designed a wire that would move back and forth in response to sound vibrations. The vibrations could then be measured. Scientists use the term hertz (Hz) to describe the frequency of a sound wave. A hertz is equal to one wave passing a certain point in one second.

Experiment #3
Rubber Band Music

↳ Does it take more energy to shout than to whisper?

You have discovered from Experiment #2 that sound vibrations cause molecules in the air to push against each other in waves. Put your hand in front of your mouth and say "Ahh!" Say it louder. Now say it softer. Do you feel a vibration on your hand? What question might we ask from this observation? Does it take more effort or energy to make a louder sound than a softer sound? Come up with

a hypothesis about energy and sound.
Here is one option: **It takes more energy to make a
louder sound than a softer sound.**

Here's what you'll need:

- An empty tissue box (one that is longer than
  it is tall)
- 2 long rubber bands that are the same size
  and thickness
- 2 thick markers

Gather the materials before you begin.

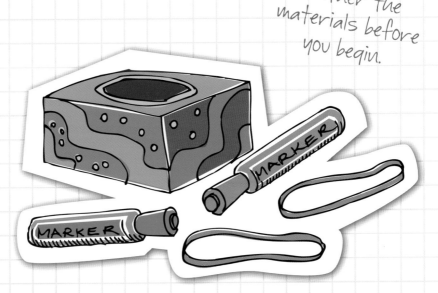

Instructions:

1. If there is a thin plastic sheet covering the hole
   in the tissue box, remove it.
2. Stretch the rubber bands around the length of
   the tissue box. Space them about 1 inch (2.5
   cm) apart. The rubber bands should be stretched
   across the hole where the tissues come out.

3. Insert the markers underneath the rubber bands so that they are resting on top of the tissue box. Slide one marker to the left. It should reach across the opening of the box but be near the edge of the hole. Move the other marker to the right until it is near the opposite edge of the hole.
4. Use your thumb and index finger to pull one rubber band up 1 inch. Let go. Observe the rubber band. What sound do you hear?
5. Now do the same with the other rubber band. Is the sound the same or different? Record your observations.
6. Now pull the first rubber band up 2 inches (5.1 cm). Let go. Is the sound louder or softer? Does the rubber band vibrate longer? Does it vibrate more intensely? Repeat with the other rubber band.
7. Try pulling the first rubber band up 3 inches (7.6 cm). What happens when you release it? How is the sound different from your previous trials? Is it louder? Repeat with the other rubber band.

Make some rubber band music!

When you speak or sing, the vocal cords in your neck vibrate as air passes over them. This creates sound waves in your nose and mouth. The sound gets louder when more air travels across the vocal cords.

Vocal cords work best when the air is leaving your lungs. Try saying "A, B, C" while breathing out. Now try saying it while breathing in. Hum your favorite song with your mouth closed. Does it work? The air is passing through your vocal cords and leaving through your nose. Try humming again with your mouth closed and your nose pinched tight. Does it work?

Conclusion:

To understand your results, you need to know a little more about sound waves. The height of a sound wave is called the amplitude. Tall sound waves have bigger amplitudes. Sounds with high amplitudes are louder. Sounds with low amplitudes are softer. In this experiment, "bigger" sound waves are those with bigger amplitudes.

Did you notice that the rubber band seemed to vibrate with more energy when it was plucked harder? Was the sound louder when the rubber band had more energy? It takes more energy to produce a loud sound. The energy carried by the sound waves of loud sounds vibrates more air molecules. The molecules are moved farther forward and backward. Does this help explain your results? Was your hypothesis correct?

Experiment #4

Change the Pitch

↖ Your vocal cords vibrate when you speak or sing.

We just learned that more energy is needed to make louder sounds. But can we change sounds in other ways? Think about what else you might already know about sound. When you shout or whisper, you change how much air you push past your vocal cords. You also know that vibrations are an important part of sound. What happens when you sing the high and low notes of a song? Do vibrations have something to do with the highness or lowness of sounds? A hypothesis could be: **Changing a vibration can make a sound higher or lower.**

Here's what you'll need:
- 4 water glasses that are the same size
- A measuring cup
- Water
- A metal spoon

Be sure the glasses are the same size.

Instructions:
1. Place the glasses on a flat work surface.
2. Use the measuring cup to pour ¼ cup of water in the first glass. Pour ½ cup of water in the second glass. Pour ¾ cup of water in the third glass. Pour 1 cup of water in the fourth glass.

3. Gently tap the side of the first glass with the metal spoon. What sound do you hear?
4. Tap the second glass. Is the sound different?
5. Tap the third glass. Pay attention to the sound it makes.
6. Tap the fourth glass. Note the sound produced. Write down your observations.

Can you play a song on your glasses?

Conclusion:

Which glass makes the highest note? Which makes the lowest note? How do vibrations play a part in the outcome of this experiment?

Hitting the glass with the spoon makes the glass vibrate. If you looked closely, you might have observed that both the glass and the water inside vibrate. The vibrating glass transfers its energy to the nearby air and water. The vibrating water also helps cause the air to vibrate. The glass with the most water makes a lower sound. The glass with the smallest amount of water makes a higher sound.

When you add water to the glass, it's as if it becomes part of the glass itself. Adding water increases the mass (the amount of physical matter something contains) of the glass. Something with a larger mass creates sounds with lower frequencies. Vibrations with lower frequencies create a lower pitch. Pitch is the highness or lowness of a sound. Did you prove your hypothesis?

Musicians use similar ideas from this experiment when they play an instrument called a glass harp. They fill many glasses with different amounts of water, to match the frequencies of the notes of a musical scale. They run their fingers around the rim of the glasses. This causes the glasses to vibrate and make different sounds. The sounds create a song!

Experiment #5
Testing the Sound Barrier

We can learn about sound by listening to an ambulance siren.

You've learned that sound travels through air. You've also learned that you can change the way a sound is made. What else do we know about sound? We know that sound can change depending on where we are standing. An ambulance siren sounds different when you are outside than when you are in the house. How are we able to hear something that is outside when we are inside? Think about it. Could sound have the ability to pass through things besides air? That leads us to our next hypothesis: **Sound waves can pass through a solid object.**

Here's what you'll need:
- Earbuds
- An MP3 player or other portable music player
- 2 empty cardboard tubes (paper towel rolls work well)
- A ceramic coffee mug

Looking for empty cardboard tubes? Check your family's recycling bin!

Instructions:
1. Plug the earbuds into the music player. Push the earpieces halfway into the length of 1 cardboard tube.

2. Turn on the music player and set the volume to low.
3. Place the free end of the first tube against one end of the second tube. You should now have one long tube.
4. Put your ear against the free end of the second tube. Can you hear music? Is it loud or soft?
5. Set the second tube aside.
6. Put the free end of the first tube inside the coffee mug. It should touch the inner base of the mug. Place one end of the second tube against the bottom of the mug on the outside. The base of the mug should now be between the two tubes.
7. Press your ear against the free end of the second tube. What do you hear? Does the sound pass through?

Listen carefully!

Conclusion:
The surface of the mug is solid. But could you still hear sounds? When sound waves cause a wall to vibrate, the air on the other side of the

wall vibrates, too. This is why sound can be heard through walls. How does this concept apply to the setup of this experiment? You could still hear music because the energy of the sound wave passed through the solid mug, from molecule to molecule. The sound waves, however, lost energy as they passed through the mug to the air on the other side. Did you prove your hypothesis?

Scientists put their knowledge of how sound works to good use. Many experts make homes and office buildings using thick walls, special materials, and specific construction methods. These help absorb the energy of sound waves and prevent the vibrations from passing to the other side of a wall—and into another room.

When sound bounces off an object, it is called an echo. Bats, dolphins, and whales use sound waves to locate objects. When the sound wave bounces back, the animal can figure out the distance and location of an object. The navy also uses sound waves to find objects under water. Special sonar equipment is used. Sound travels faster in water than in air. Sonar does not work in space. There are no air molecules to carry the sound waves.

Experiment #6

Do It Yourself!

Scientists measure the amount of energy in sound waves in units called decibels. We call this the volume. Scientists experiment with different ways to make it easier for the human ear to hear soft sounds or block out loud ones.

Have you ever noticed that cupping your hand behind your ear can help you hear something? Your hand kind of makes a cone shape. Could holding the smaller end of a cone to your

Design my own experiment? Sounds good to me!

ear make it easier to pick up sounds? How? Is it somehow able to catch more sound waves? Does it direct them toward your ear? To find out, set up an experiment. What is your hypothesis? What materials would you need to make a paper cone and run the experiment? Write out the instructions for your experiment. How many soft sounds can you hear without the cone? How many with the cone? Write down what you find out.

Okay, scientists! Now you know many new things about sound. You learned through your observations and experiments. You also found out that even though you can't see sound waves, they can be used to do a lot of important things. And you discovered that you, too, can be a scientist and create sound experiments of your own!

GLOSSARY

conclusion (kuhn-KLOO-zhuhn) a final decision, thought, or opinion

decibels (DESS-uh-belz) units used to measure the energy in a sound wave and describe how loud a sound is

echo (EK-oh) a sound that bounces off an object and returns to your ears

frequency (FREE-kwuhn-see) the number of sound waves that pass a location in a specific amount of time

hertz (HURTS) a unit used to measure the frequency of the vibrations of sound waves; 1 hertz is 1 sound wave per second

hypothesis (hy-POTH-uh-sihss) a logical guess about what will happen in an experiment

method (METH-uhd) a way of doing something

observations (ob-zur-VAY-shuhnz) things that are seen or noticed with one's senses

sonar (SOH-nar) a device that sends sound waves through water and detects when they bounce off of something

FOR MORE INFORMATION

BOOKS

Bayrock, Fiona. *Sound: A Question and Answer Book*. Mankato, MN: Capstone Press, 2006.

Landau, Elaine. *The Sense of Hearing*. New York: Children's Press, 2009.

Making Sense of Senses. New York: Children's Press, 2008.

WEB SITES

BBC—Science: Physics: Hearing

www.bbc.co.uk/schools/ks3bitesize/science/physics/sound_4.shtml

Learn more about your ears and hearing

KidsHealth—Experiments to Try: Do You Hear What I Hear?

kidshealth.org/kid/closet/experiments/experiment_hear.html

For a fun sound activity to try with a friend

PBS Kids—ZOOMsci: String Telephone

pbskids.org/zoom/activities/sci/stringtelephone.html

Use your science skills to make and test a telephone

INDEX

About the → Author

Christine Taylor-Butler is a freelance author with degrees in both civil engineering and art and design from MIT. When Christine is not writing, she is reading, drawing, or looking for unusual new science ideas to try. She is the author of more than 40 fiction and nonfiction books for children.